Meanings into Words
Intermediate

Test Book

Meanings into Words
Intermediate

An integrated course for students of English

Test Book

Adrian Doff, Christopher Jones and
Keith Mitchell

Cambridge University Press

Cambridge
London   New York   New Rochelle
Melbourne   Sydney

Published by the Press Syndicate of the University of Cambridge
The Pitt Building, Trumpington Street, Cambridge CB2 1RP
32 East 57th Street, New York, NY 10022, USA
296 Beaconsfield Parade, Middle Park, Melbourne 3206, Australia

© Cambridge University Press 1983

First published 1983

Drawings by Chris Evans

Printed in Great Britain at the
University Press, Cambridge

ISBN 0 521 28285 3 Test Book
ISBN 0 521 28283 7 Student's Book
ISBN 0 521 28286 1 Teacher's Book
ISBN 0 521 28284 5 Workbook
ISBN 0 521 23887 0 Cassette (Student's Book)
ISBN 0 521 23888 9 Cassette (Drills)

MU

Contents

Progress Test   Units 1 – 4

DO NOT WRITE IN THIS BOOK

---

1   SENTENCE REWRITING   *10 marks*

Rewrite these sentences, using the word in brackets, so that they mean the same.

Example Perhaps I won't have spaghetti again tonight. (**think**)
Answer   I don't think I'll have spaghetti again tonight.

1 The hospital's got 30 beds. (**there**)
2 Monkton Garage usually services my car for me. (**have**)
3 Her employers often send her to the United States. (**gets**)
4 Keep on as far as the chemist's, and then turn right. (**until**)
5 The company publishes a report every six months. (**year**)

---

2   ASKING QUESTIONS   *12 marks*

Write questions for these answers.

Example I live in London.
Answer   Where do you live?

1 ...... ?   I clean them every day.
2 ...... ?   Yes, there's one under the window.
3 ...... ?   It takes me about 50 minutes.
4 ...... ?   I'm not sure – I'm thinking of getting a Citroen.
5 ...... ?   The hospital? Go on up this road, and you'll see it on your left.
6 ...... ?   Sausage and chips, usually.

---

3   GAP-FILLING   *7 marks*

Fill these gaps with a suitable word or phrase.

Example The rain came in ...... a hole in the roof.
Answer   through

1 She lives in a flat ...... the fourth floor.
2 I usually watch TV in the evening, but ...... I go to the pub.
3 I never see him, but he writes to me now and ....

4 He walked straight ...... me, without even saying 'Hello'.
5 There are boutiques, ... sell all the latest fashions.
6 He came ...... me and shook my hand.
7 She took 10 pence ...... her pocket.

4 VOCABULARY   *9 marks*

Answer each of these questions with a word or phrase.

1 Who do you pay *rent* to?

2 What do you call someone who
  a) sweeps roads?
  b) tests people's eyes?
  c) designs buildings?

3 What do these people do?
  a) a cashier?
  b) a plumber?

4 Write *two* places where you can:
  a) follow your cultural interests
  b) take your children for a day out
  c) stay for a few nights

5 COMPOSITION   *12 marks*

Choose *three* of the topics below, and write about 30 words (two or three
sentences) on each one.

1 Describe the room where you are now.
2 Tell someone how to get to the toilet from where you are now.
3 What are your plans for the weekend?
4 Where do you have lunch, and what do you have?
5 Look at this diagram of a simple bell-pull and say how it works.

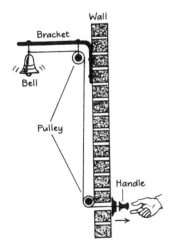

Total marks: 50   *Time: one lesson (45–50 minutes)*

Progress Test   Units 5 – 8

DO NOT WRITE IN THIS BOOK

---

1   SENTENCE REWRITING   *14 marks*

Rewrite these sentences, beginning with the words given, so that they mean the same.

Example   Charles Dickens wrote *Oliver Twist*.
            Oliver Twist......
Answer   *Oliver Twist* was written by Charles Dickens.

1 I was 30 before I visited France.
   I didn't ......
2 Don't talk in the library, please.
   Would you mind......
3 The Red Cross is flying medical supplies into the war zone.
   Medical supplies......
4 'Can I borrow your camera, Paul?' asked Fiona.
   Fiona asked Paul......
5 He's still looking for a flat.
   He hasn't......
6 Nobody's using the kitchen at the moment.
   There......
7 'You can use my telephone if you like, Ken,' said Beryl.
   Beryl offered......

---

2   MAKING SENTENCES   *8 marks*

Write full sentences from the prompts below.

Example   The Opera House / build / 1843.
Answer   The Opera House was built in 1843.

1 Henry / born / 4 o'clock / morning / Tuesday / 18 May.
2 Church / design / Sir Thomas Woolley / Middle Ages.
3 His first novel / publish / turn / century.
4 Year / after / leave / college / Mona / emigrate / Australia.

3 MAKING REQUESTS AND OFFERS   *6 marks*

Make appropriate requests and offers. Use a different expression each time.

1 Ask a friend to give you a newspaper.
2 Ask a stranger to help you carry your luggage.
3 Ask your landlady for permission to give a party in her house.
4 Ask a friend for permission to use his phone.
5 Offer your friend a lift in your car.
6 Offer to collect a parcel for someone.

4 RECENT ACTIVITIES AND ACHIEVEMENTS   *10 marks*

Peter is unemployed. From the notes below, write sentences saying what he **has been doing**, what he **has done**, and what he **did**.

1 Peter / try / find / job.
2 He / look / advertisements / newspapers / and / so far / he / apply for / six jobs.
3 But / he / not / receive / any replies / yet.
4 He / also / visit / local factories / over / past few days.
5 Yesterday / he / have / interview / at / shoe factory / but / he / not / be offered / job.
6 Now / he / decide / put / advertisement / in / newspaper / himself.

5 COMPOSITION   *12 marks*

Choose *three* of the topics below, and write about 30 words (two or three sentences) on each one.

1 *either* What is happening in your country at the moment?
  or   What is your brother/sister/mother/father doing these days?
2 Choose someone you know something about. Give a brief outline of his/her career.
3 Give some important facts about your country's history or your town's history.
4 Write about your activities and achievements over the past few weeks.

Total marks: 50   *Time: one lesson (45–50 minutes)*

Progress Test   Units 9 – 12

DO NOT WRITE IN THIS BOOK

---
1   SENTENCE REWRITING   *8 marks*

Rewrite these sentences, using the word in brackets, so that they mean the same.

Example Perhaps I won't have spaghetti again tonight. (**think**)
Answer   I don't think I'll have spaghetti again tonight.

1 He didn't use to go to the theatre very much, but now he often goes. (**than**)
2 He likes spending money more than he likes earning money. (**prefers**)
3 I love people taking my photograph. (**having**)
4 I was having breakfast when I heard the news. (**while**)

---
2   COMPARISON   *6 marks*

From the prompts below, write comparative sentences. Begin with the first word(s) given.

1 Poodles / greyhounds (**run**). Poodles......
2 India / Saudi Arabia (**population**). India......
3 Nurses / doctors (**money**). Nurses......
4 Corner shops / supermarkets (**shop at**). Corner shops......

---
3   CHANGES   *6 marks*

Look at the two
pictures, which show
how a street used to
be and how it is
now.
Write sentences
saying what has
happened to:
1 the café
2 the trees
3 the cottage
4 the cobbled street

The table shows how much Paul likes various things.

Example Paul doesn't like swimming.

Write sentences showing how much he likes doing the other six things. Use a *different* verb each time.

	No!	No	–	Yes	Yes!
swim		✓			
write letters			✓		
be laughed at	✓				
do housework	✓				
eat garlic					✓
wake up late					✓
play golf				✓	

---

5 GAP-FILLING   *12 marks*

Complete the sentences below, so that they make sense.

1 I can't hear a word you're saying. Can't you ......?
2 A: Come on! Hurry up!
   B: Give me a chance! I'm ...... I can!
3 I ...... keep fit. I go running every morning and evening.
4 I could see them .... They obviously didn't want anyone to hear what they were saying.
5 ...... while .... He was taken to hospital immediately.
6 I remember my mother ...... from school every afternoon.
7 Mount Everest is ...... in the world.
8 Where ...... to go for your holidays when you were young?
9 He ...... when suddenly the handle fell off.
10 She's got her own flat now; she doesn't ....
11 I spend quite a lot, but not as much ....

---

6 COMPOSITION   *12 marks*

Choose *three* of the topics below, and write about 30 words (two or three sentences) on each one.

1 *either* Which do you prefer: eating at home or eating out? Why?
   or   Say what you like and don't like about going to the dentist.
2 What do you remember about the things you used to do as a child? Write *either* about birthdays *or* about going to bed.
3 *either* How have you changed over the past five years?
   or   How much easier has travelling become over the last 20 years?
4 Describe an incident when you were frightened. Say what happened, and in what circumstances.

Total marks: 50   *Time: one lesson (45–50 minutes)*

Progress Test   Units 13 – 16

DO NOT WRITE IN THIS BOOK

1   SENTENCE REWRITING
14 *marks*

Rewrite these sentences, beginning with the words given, so that they mean the same.

Example   Charles Dickens wrote *Oliver Twist*.
            Oliver Twist......
Answer   *Oliver Twist* was written by Charles Dickens.

1 You should have it repaired.
  If I ......
2 He climbs mountains quite a lot.
  He does ......
3 She advised me to take an aspirin.
  She suggested ......
4 She plays the piano quite well.
  She's ......

5 You don't drive as well as I do.
  I'm better ......
6 I moved into this house when I got married, and I'm still living here.
  I've ......
7 I haven't seen them for ages.
  It's ......

2   GIVING REASONS FOR ADVICE
6 *marks*

Give *two* different reasons for each of these pieces of advice. Use the words given.

1 You ought to reserve a seat on the train.
  a) otherwise   b) in case
2 It's Friday. You ought to go to the bank.
  a) so that   b) otherwise

3 You ought to take a gun with you.
  a) in case   b) so that

3   LOCATION
6 *marks*

Complete these sentences with a suitable word or phrase.

1 There's someone ...... the door. Go and see who it is.
2 You'll find the ice compartment ...... the refrigerator.
3 Do you mind if I sit ...... you?
4 The bullet made a hole ...... of the car.
5 The café is ...... the river. ⎫
6 The boathouse is ...... the café. ⎬ (see map)

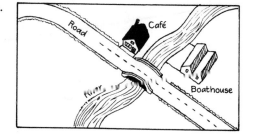

12

7–9 Look at the map and write *three* different sentences describing exactly where Town A is. Begin 'Town A ......'

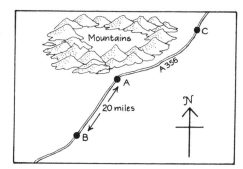

4 GAP-FILLING

6 marks

Complete the sentences below, so that they make sense.

1 A: Have ...... ?
   B: No, I haven't, but I was once bitten by a dog.
2 A: I can't go to sleep.
   B: ...... ?
   A: Yes I have, but it didn't help.
3 I like your watch. How long have ...... ?

4 You go to evening classes, do you? How long ...... ?
5 My car's terribly dirty. I haven't ...... April!
6 A: ...... ?
   B Yoga? No, I don't, actually.

5 VOCABULARY

6 marks

1 If you go hill-walking, what should you:
   a) use to find where north is?
   b) wear on your feet?
   c) wear to keep your body warm and dry?
   d) listen to before you leave?
2 What do you call a girl who stays with a family abroad and helps with the housework?

3 What do you call:
   a) a place where a road crosses a railway?
   b) the line that divides the world into northern and southern hemispheres?
   c) the line between two countries?
   d) the place where a river goes into the sea?
4 Write the names of:
   a) two indoor games
   b) two ways of keeping fit
   c) two leisure activities which involve *making* things

6 COMPOSITION

12 marks

Choose *three* of the topics below, and write about 30 words (two or three sentences) on each one.

1 Write about two of your leisure activities: say how much you do of each one, and how good you are at it.
2 Choose a tourist resort in your country, and describe exactly where it is.

3 Give some advice to someone who's going to take his/her driving test.
4 Write about your oldest possession. Say how long you've had it, and exactly how you first got it.

Total marks: 50

Time: one lesson (45–50 minutes)

Progress Test   Units 17 – 20

DO NOT WRITE IN THIS BOOK

---

1   PREDICTION   *6 marks*

Rewrite these remarks using the words given in brackets.

1 John and Mary will get married soon. (**think**)
2 You'll get on very well together. (**expect**)
3 You won't have to work very hard. (**doubt**)

4 They won't offer him the job. (**definitely**)
5 The miners will go on strike. (**probably**)
6 He'll try to borrow some money. (**might**)

---

2   SIMILARITIES   *5 marks*

Respond to the remarks below in *two* ways, using **too, so, either, neither / nor**.

1 I've got a Japanese girlfriend.
2 I can't stand men with beards.
3 My brother's in the army.

4 I went to the Film Festival.
5 My name wasn't on the list.

---

3   OBLIGATION   *6 marks*

Fill the gaps with a suitable obligation or permission verb.

Example In most countries people over 18 ...... vote.
Answer   can

1 You ...... stand up if you don't want to.
2 Children ...... to drive cars or motorcycles.
3 If you go abroad, you ...... take your passport.
4 People who don't earn any money ...... pay income tax.
5 We ...... have guests in our rooms, but they ...... leave by 10 o'clock in the evening.

---

4   DEFINITIONS   *5 marks*

Define each of the things below using a relative clause.

1 football boots
2 a waterproof coat
3 an automatic cooker

4 a waiting room
5 a bread knife

14

5 GAP-FILLING   *8 marks*

Complete the sentences below, so that they make sense.

1 Quick! Where's the bathroom? I think ...... be sick!
2 I'm afraid I can't see you tomorrow afternoon. I ...... my wife from the airport
   then.
3 ...... coffee ...... cigarettes are very good for you in large quantities.
4 A: Have you got any of that stuff ...... ?
   B: You mean correcting fluid – yes, here you are.
5 Is ...... of your sisters married? Yes, one of them is.
6 It's none of my business who you marry. You can marry ....
7 A: What sort of penknife do you want?
   B: I want ...... a corkscrew.
8 A: I can stay out as late as I want.
   B: What? You mean your parents ...... go home before midnight?

6 VOCABULARY   *8 marks*

1 What do you get from: a) a mine? b) a percolator?
2 What do ants and butterflies have in common?
3 Where might you find:
   a) a strap?
   b) a pendulum?
   c) a plug?
   d) a serrated edge?
4 Write *two* kinds of:
   a) basket
   b) board
   c) pot
   d) brush

7 COMPOSITION   *12 marks*

Choose *three* of the topics below, and write about 30 words (two or three
sentences) on each one.

1 *either* Do you think the world's population will continue to grow at its
            present rate?
   or   What do you think will have happened by the end of the century?
2 Compare two cities you know. In what ways are they similar? In what ways
   are they different?
3 You were staying in a hotel last week, and you left *either* a coat *or* a handbag
   in your room.
   Write part of a letter to the manager describing it.
4 What restrictions are (and are not) placed on you during examinations?

Total marks: 50   *Time: one lesson (45–50 minutes)*

Progress Test   Units 21 – 24

DO NOT WRITE IN THIS BOOK

---
1   SENTENCE REWRITING   *10 marks*

Rewrite these sentences, using the words in brackets, so that they mean the same.

Example   Perhaps I won't have spaghetti again tonight. (**think**)
Answer   I don't think I'll have spaghetti again tonight.

1 The water was so cold that we couldn't swim in it. (**enough**)
2 The examination was very easy – I left after 20 minutes. (**such**)
3 The purpose of 'Spokes' is to improve conditions for cyclists. (**concerned**)
4 She looks strange, but she's a very ordinary person. (**in spite of**)
5 When I arrived, everyone in the house was awake. (**wake up**)

---
2   CRITICISING   *15 marks*

Write *two* sentences for each situation
a) criticising the person using **should(n't)**
b) explaining your criticism using **If......**

1 Albert eats a lot, so he's fat.
2 Felicity doesn't put things away, so she's always losing things.
3 Sid forgot to set his alarm, so he didn't catch the train.
4 Cynthia was throwing bricks at passing cars, so she was arrested.
5 Anthony wasn't watching the milk, so it boiled over.

---
3   DESCRIBING A SCENE   *5 marks*

This is what you saw
when you looked out
of the window
yesterday. Say what
you saw. Talk about:
1 the cat
2 the ladder
3 the fireman
4 the neighbours
5 the dogs

4 GAP-FILLING

Complete the sentences below so that they make sense.

1 He's got some terrible habits. He ...... his fingernails.
2 Because it ...... south, the room was warm and sunny.
3 The restaurant was empty – all the guests ...... some time before.
4 ...... is to warn people about the dangers of smoking.
5 Birds migrate ...... find food in warmer climates.
6 Despite ...... , the Government was re-elected.
7 As a result ...... a lot of people have decided to sell their cars.
8 He recognised me because ...... the week before.

5 COMPOSITION

Choose *three* of the topics below and write about 30 words (two or three sentences) on each one.

1 *either* You stayed at an awful hotel last summer. Say what was wrong with it.
   or   Describe what annoys you about any member of your family.
2 Recently you visited *either* the scene of an accident *or* a very busy restaurant. Describe what you saw when you arrived.
3 What problems are caused by *either* television *or* overpopulation?
4 Describe the purpose(s) of *either* schools *or* the Red Cross.

Total marks: 50   *Time: one lesson (45–50 minutes)*

Final Achievement Test

DO NOT WRITE IN THIS BOOK

I MULTIPLE CHOICE
20 marks

Choose (a), (b), (c) or (d) to complete the sentences below.

1 His desk is ...... the office.
   a) at back of   b) at the back of   c) in back of   d) in the back of

2 I ...... in 1970.
   a) born   b) was born   c) am born   d) have been born

3 'I haven't been to Russia.'
   a) Nor have I   b) Nor I have   c) So haven't I   d) So I haven't

4 Collect me at 8 o'clock. I ...... my bath by then.
   a) will have   b) will be having   c) will have had   d) will have been having

5 Are you any good ...... ?
   a) playing chess   b) at playing chess   c) in playing chess
   d) chess player

6 Take my address ...... you want to write to me.
   a) in case   b) in the case   c) in any case   d) in that case

7 He doesn't enjoy ....
   a) to be shouted at him   b) to be shouted at   c) being shouted at him
   d) being shouted at

8 It was ...... nice day that I lay in the garden all afternoon.
   a) so   b) such   c) so a   d) such a

9 We had to stop ...... the traffic lights because they were red.
   a) in   b) on   c) at   d) by

10 They do ...... skating.
   a) quite a lot of   b) quite a lot   c) quite much of   d) quite much

11 Of course he was offended – you shouldn't ...... him when he came in.
   a) ignore   b) be ignoring   c) have ignored   d) have been ignoring

12 If you've got 'flu, you ...... go to work.
   a) had better not   b) had better not to   c) would better not
   d) would better not to

13 I expect there'll be plenty to eat – you ...... bring any food.
   a) needn't   b) needn't to   c) mustn't   d) mustn't to

14 Now I can go home. I ...... all my work.
   a) finished   b) was finishing   c) have finished   d) have been finishing

15 You can work much ...... than that.
     a) hardly   b) more hardly   c) harder   d) more harder

16 I don't suppose I could have a sandwich, ... ?
     a) don't I   b) do I   c) couldn't I   d) could I

17 If you ...... more time outside, you'd be much fitter.
     a) spend   b) spent   c) would spend   d) have spent

18 I've known him ...... three years.
     a) during   b) in   c) for   d) since

19 I'm tired. I ...... do any more work.
     a) think I won't   b) think I wouldn't   c) don't think I'll
     d) don't think I'd

20 He dances well ....
     a) in spite he has a bad leg   b) in spite his bad leg   c) in spite of he has a bad leg
     d) in spite of his bad leg

2 SENTENCE REWRITING   *20 marks*

Rewrite the sentences below so that they mean the same. Begin with the words
given.

1   The au pair girl is looking after the children.
    The children......
2   I don't swim as well as I used to.
    I used to be......
3   I don't mind how long you stay.
    You can......
4   His cell was so small that he couldn't lie down.
    There wasn't enough......
5   The last time my eyes were tested was in 1967.
    I haven't......

Rewrite the sentences below, using the words in brackets, so that they mean the
same.

6   I advised him to complain to the police. (**suggested**)
7   You didn't hear what I said because you weren't paying attention. (**if**)
8   Could you stop blowing smoke in my face? (**mind**)
9   I like giving presents more than I like being given presents. (**prefer**)
10 You probably won't be paid very well. (**doubt**)

⟫→

3 WRITING A LETTER 20 marks

Below is part of a letter in note form. Write each sentence, putting the verbs in the correct form, and adding any other necessary words.

1   We / now / in Turkey / probably / arrive / Istanbul / tomorrow.
2   We / both / very tired / as / we / travel / non-stop / three days.
3   Perhaps / we / shouldn't / drive / so far / such / short time.
4   Yesterday / too tired / concentrate / properly / nearly / have / accident.
5   It / happen / while / we / drive / empty road / north coast / Greece.
6   Lorry / suddenly / come out / side turning / in front / us.
7   Richard / brake / hard / he can / we / stop / grass / side / road.
8   If / brakes / not / work / properly / we / go / straight / into / side / lorry.
9   We / both / scared / we / decide / sell / car.
10 We / continue / journey / Istanbul / train!

4 GAP-FILLING 12 marks

Complete the sentences below, so that they make sense.

1   A: ......?
    B: Oh, I have it done about once a month, usually.
2   A: How long ......?
    B: Oh, I haven't been there for over a year.
3   It isn't an antique shop any more – it's been ...... a café.
4   If you ...... , you wouldn't have to keep going to the dentist.
5   A: ...... ?
    B: It's very kind of you, but I'd rather walk, thank you.
6   Have you found a job yet, or are you ...... ?
7   I'm sorry I haven't come to see you before, but I ...... over the last few weeks.
8   An oven-proof dish is a dish ...... in a hot oven.
9   Don't worry about your cat, Mrs Johnson. ...... soon.
10 You should put a lock on your bicycle. Otherwise ....
11 When I met him again a month later, he'd ...... that I didn't recognise him at first.
12 As a result of ...... lots of people have decided to give it up.

5 VOCABULARY 8 marks

1 What would you do at these places?
   a)   a newsagent's
   b)   a lost property office
   c)   a call box

2 What would you use to:
   a)   hold luggage on a car roof?
   b)   cut the grass in your garden?
   c)   play chess on?
   d)   catch mice?

3 What do you call someone who:
   a) cleans windows?
   b) plays the guitar?
   c) keeps knocking things over?
   d) talks about himself all the time?

4 Give verbs that mean:
   a) to move on your hands and knees
   b) to break into a conversation
   c) to go running to keep fit
   d) to travel by stopping passing cars
   e) to paint a room, put new paper on the walls, etc.

6 COMPOSITION   *20 marks*

Write a short paragraph (about 30 words) about each of the following.

1 *either* Describe a famous building in your town.
  or   Describe your cooker.
2 *either* What did you do last night after leaving school/work?
  or   What is the earliest thing you remember?
3 *either* How have fashions changed in the last five years?
  or   What have you been doing recently?
4 Give some advice, with reasons, to someone who is:
  either going for an interview for a job
  or   going sailing

Total marks: 100   *Time: two lessons (90–100 minutes)*